> Fear, Jacqueline
>   Apache family. – (Beans)
>   1. Apache Indians – Social life and customs –
>   Juvenile literature   2. Albuquerque (New Mexico)
>   – Social life and customs – Juvenile literature
>   I. Title
>   978.9'61   E99.A6
>   ISBN 0-7136-2716-6

A & C Black (Publishers) Limited
35 Bedford Row, London WC1R 4JH

© 1985 text Jacqueline Fear
© 1985 photographs Sally Fear

Acknowledgements
The map is by Tony Garrett

All rights reserved. No part of this publication may be reproduced, stored in a retrieval system, or transmitted in any form or by any means, electronic, mechanical, photocopying, recording or otherwise, without the prior permission of A & C Black (Publishers) Limited.

ISBN 0-7136-2716-6

Filmset by August Filmsetting, Haydock, St Helens
Printed in Hong Kong by Dai Nippon Printing Co. Ltd

Apache Family

Jacqueline Fear

Photographs by Sally Fear

A & C Black · London

Hi, my name is Reba June Serafin. I'm ten years old and I live with my parents in Albuquerque, New Mexico.

You probably haven't heard the name Reba before. It's made up from the first letters of my two grandmothers' names, Rebecca and Edith, and two of my aunts' names, Betty and Alberta.

My family is Apache and my parents grew up on the Jicarilla Apache Reservation. Both my grandmas still live there. The reservation is in New Mexico, about 290 kilometres north of Albuquerque. Before our land was invaded by the Whiteman, the Apache roamed all over the plains. The land we have now was reserved for our tribe by the President of the United States about a hundred years ago.

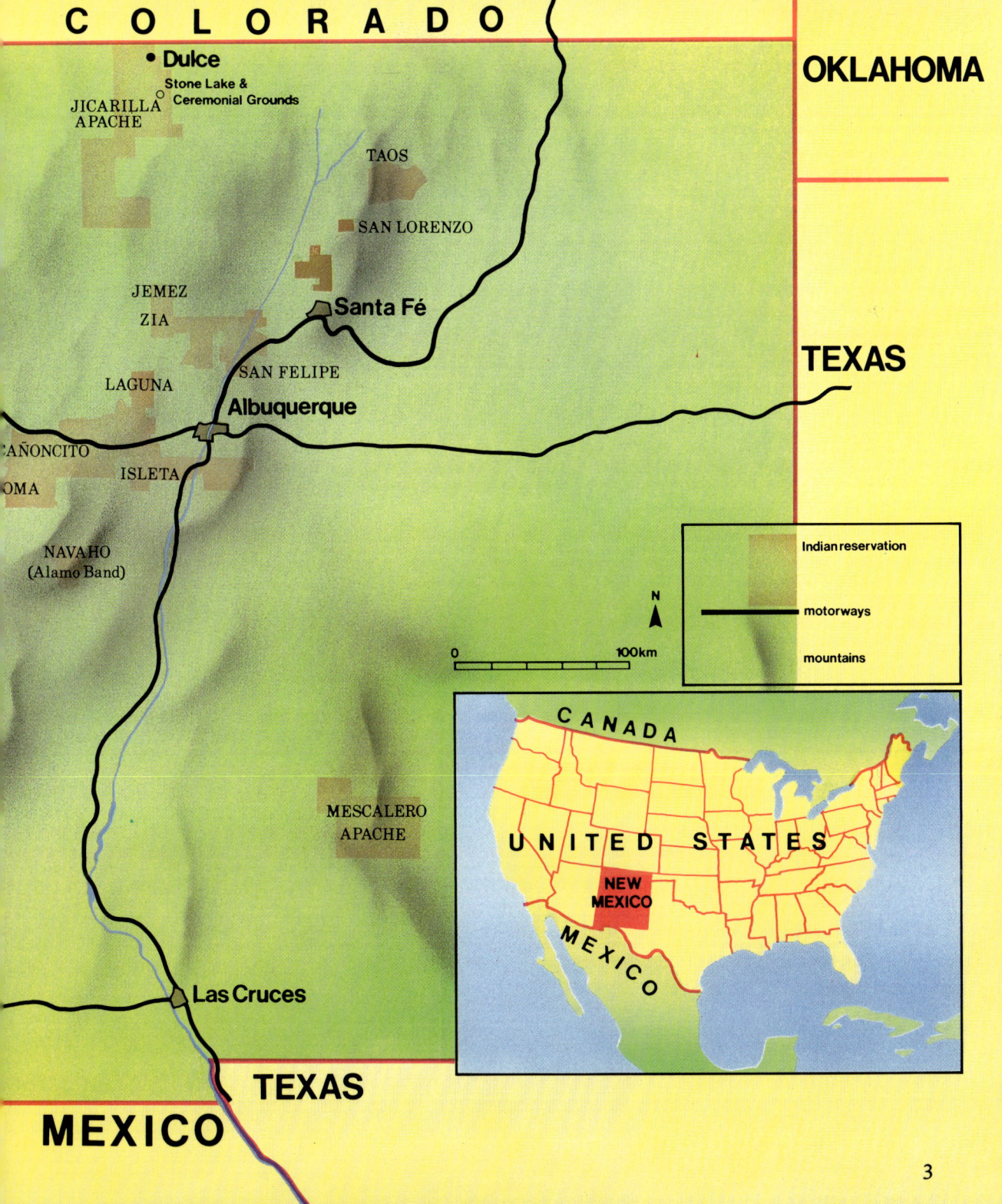

That's me with Mum and Dad outside our house. I'm holding my cat Scary. I call him Scary because he runs away from everyone. Grandma calls him Musha. That's Apache for cat. When we brought him home from Grandma's he was still wild.

At the back of the house we have a paddock where we keep our horses. My horse is called O'del, Mum's is called Whiskey, and Dad's is called Mo.

We also have another horse which is too old to be ridden, and a colt called Jet. Jet is two years old and he's a thoroughbred. When we're both a little older, he'll be my horse.

There's no grass in the paddock because the weather is too hot and dry. Twice a day, Dad has to feed the horses with hay. My job is to feed our two dogs. They're called Bear and Foxy. They live outside in the yard because they're guard dogs. When I get home from school, I often unchain them so that we can play together. I'm taking Bear to dog-training classes, but he isn't very obedient yet.

Most mornings, my dad is the first to get up. While he's cooking breakfast, I go down to the mail box to see if there are any letters for us. The mail box is outside the house in the street, so the mailman can make all his deliveries without leaving his van.

My dad works for the US Post Office. At work, he has to sort all the mail ready for the next delivery.

Some packages are too big to go into people's mail boxes. Dad puts the big packages into lockers in the mail room. The locker keys are delivered to people's mail boxes, so that they can collect their packages.

Mum used to go out to work but this year she gave up her job to study. She's taking a degree in accountancy and business studies at the University of Albuquerque. Mum has to study other subjects too. Today she has an American History class. They're learning about how George Washington fought to help the USA win independence from the English .

I go to the Catholic School in Albuquerque. It's not far from Dad's Post Office, so he drives me to school on his way to work. The journey takes about twenty five minutes.

School starts at 8.15 in the morning. At the beginning of school, we pledge allegiance to the United States of America. We all stand up and salute the flag. Then lessons start.

We have lessons in English, Maths, Geography, History and Physical Training. Today in English we're having a spelling test. Spelling is my best subject.

At the back of our classroom, there's a shelf where we all leave our lunch boxes. At break there's always a rush to get there first.

I sit with my best friend Theresa at lunch. We sometimes swap things to eat. Mum's packed my favourite, potato chips, and I've ordered chocolate milk at school.

After our lunch break we're having PT. At the beginning of the year, our coach timed us all running one circuit round the yard. She's going to time us again at the end of the year to see if we've improved our speeds.

As soon as I get home from school, I like to go riding. When my cousin Emily comes to stay, she borrows my Mum's horse, Whiskey. I have lots of cousins living nearby. In Apache, we call our cousins brothers and sisters.

I sometimes have chores to do after school, like helping Mum with the laundry. Most of the time we can't hang the laundry out to dry because the sun is so fierce that it bleaches the clothes.

I help Dad with the garbage, too. He burns a lot of it in the yard. But we save the coke and beer cans because the metal can be used again. I sort out the cans and bottles and then ride with Dad to the dump in the pick-up truck.

The dump is across the other side of Albuquerque. The city is very spread out and all the buildings are low and far apart. You can always work out where you are though, because the mountains are East of the city.

Every two weeks, I make a list of all the groceries we have to shop for. After school, my mum and I drive to the supermarket. It's quite a long way from where we live, but the prices are cheaper there.

Outside the supermarket there's a huge car park so that people can load their groceries straight into their cars. There aren't many buses in Albuquerque, so most people drive cars.

Most weekends we put the horses in the trailer and drive to a rodeo. At the rodeo there are lots of competitions to test riding and herding skills.

We usually meet up with Uncle Bobby and Aunty Betty, and my cousins Bobbie-Nell and Blaire. Little Blaire is too young to walk yet, but she's already learning to ride.

In the rodeo, I ride in the barrels event. Three barrels are placed in a triangle and I have to ride around each one as fast as possible and gallop back to the starting line. The rider with the fastest time is the winner.

Uncle Bobby and Dad do the team roping competitions together. They have to rope a calf. My dad ropes the head and then Uncle Bobby ropes the heels.

The fastest team wins the competition. The prize is usually money and the winner is always given a special buckle.

Dad and Uncle Bobby have won quite a collection of buckles. They both learned herding on the reservation when they were young.

Now they have to practise roping in the evening after work. Uncle Bobby has some cattle, but he also has a mechanical calf to practise with. It's called a Handy Heeler.

Today, my grandma and my cousin Natalie are visiting from Dulce, the town on the reservation. They're down in Albuquerque to see the New Mexico State Fair. The fair is held here every year, and we're given a day off from school to go there.

Grandma thinks that we should eat plenty before we go, so she's making some tortillas. They're a kind of bread which you fry. We eat them with eggs and chilli sauce.

Chilli is the main crop grown in New Mexico. I love Grandma's tortillas, but Natalie and I don't like chilli. It burns your mouth.

14

At the fair there are exhibitions of all the things which people do in New Mexico. There are cattle and sheep shows, galleries of paintings, horse races and, every evening, there's a rodeo.

There's a special 'Indian Day' when Indian people can go to the fair free. At the fair there's an Indian village where you can see different Indian arts and crafts. There are displays of Indian dancing, too.

One of the Navaho Indians is making a sand painting. It's made by grinding up different coloured rocks. The paintings are usually made as part of a healing ceremony for someone who is sick. At the end of the day, the painting is always destroyed so that the Navaho gods won't be angry.

Cecilia Harrina is a Jicarilla Apache from our reservation. She's showing me how to make a basket. The Jicarilla were given their name by the Spanish who invaded our lands in the sixteenth century. It means 'little basket maker'. The Jicarilla are still famous for their basket weaving.

When we're at the fair, Mum, Dad and Grandma talk to each other in Apache. I can understand some Apache, but I can't follow everything. Sometimes, Dad starts telling a joke in English and just when he gets to the punch line, he says it in Apache. Dad says that some Apache jokes just don't work when you say them in English.

This year, I'm riding in the horse show at the State Fair. I had to win a lot of county events to qualify. The riding competitions are held inside a big building.

There's a special paddock outside where we ride the horses round to warm them up.

I keep all the rosettes which we have won at horse shows on a pinboard in my bedroom.

Some weekends we drive up to Dulce to stay with my grandma and visit our relatives there.

As soon as we arrive at Grandma's house, I like to go with my cousins to the play rock. This is a place where the rock is so soft that you can carve it. We've made a dressing-table, and a television set.

We never go up there on our own because of the rattle snakes. If I see a hole in the ground, I keep away in case it's a snake hole.

One of the rocks up here looks just like a potato, so we call it Potato Rock. From Potato Rock there's a good view of the reservation.

You can see some of the oil pumps working. The oil was discovered about thirty years ago and the money from the oil wells is very important to our tribe.

Grandma runs cattle on the reservation. Whenever the cattle are being herded, Emily and I go up to Potato Rock with binoculars.

When we can see that the men are bringing the herd near, we go back to Grandma's house and put on our red and yellow jackets so that we can be seen easily. Then we go down to the road and stop the traffic to let the cattle over.

When I stay with Grandma in the summer, we go collecting pine nuts and sugar flowers. Grandma knows how to use all sorts of different plants as medicine.

September 15th is an important date for the Jicarilla Apache. It's when we hold our annual Gojiya ceremony. We have a big feast and a relay race.

There are two clans in the Jicarilla Apache tribe – the Red clan and the White clan. They run against each other in the race. We belong to the White clan. Everyone tries to get back to the reservation for Gojiya.

The ceremonial grounds are at Stone Lake, on the reservation. Some days before Gojiya we go to Stone Lake to prepare for the celebrations and make camp.

We pitch tents and tipis (teepees) next to our shelter. Every family has a shelter near the race track. The shelters face East, towards the rising sun, like all Apache homes.

The wooden frame of the shelter remains standing from year to year. But the brushwood covering has to be repaired. We pull off the dead branches from last year and collect new oak branches.

We have to make several trips before Grandma is satisfied. Grandma (Mum's mother) is head of our camp.

For as long as anyone can remember, it has never rained for the ceremonial race. But this year, when we get up on September 15th, it's raining. Dad and Uncle Bobby have to put chains on the pick-up truck to pull the horse trailers out of the mud.

I help Grandma to chop some wood, and light a fire to cook breakfast. We all look very funny because we've made raincoats from black garbage bags.

By mid-day the rain has stopped and we can go down to the race track. The two teams of runners are in their kivas preparing for the race.

The kiva is our religious building. The White clan has a kiva at one end of the race track and the Red clan has a kiva at the other end. We worship there before the race. The two teams pray and sing and put on paint.

The two clans parade down the race track with flags and drums. Then the race begins.

In the old days the race lasted all day, until one side gave up. Nowadays, it ends when one clan is two lengths of the track ahead. The winners then start to beat their drum.

We cheer the White runners but, no matter how hard we cheer, our team is falling behind. When we hear the Red drum beating we know that, this year, we have lost the race.

When the race is over, the two clans meet in the middle of the race track. We pay the gods by throwing fruit, corn, and chilli. One year I was hit by a water melon! Afterwards, we go into our kiva and pray to the gods to protect our tribe. The elders paint our faces and hair with pollen and chalk, and give us each an eagle feather for good luck.

After the ceremony we all visit each others' camps. Everyone keeps a fire burning all day so that there is always a stew or pot of soup ready to offer to guests. In the evening, we pack up. Another Gojiya has ended. The ceremonial grounds will be empty now, until next year.

Glossary

Indian   In the fifteenth century, Europeans landed in America thinking that it was India. They called the people they found living there Indians. The name Indian stuck, even after the Europeans realised that America was a different continent.

Reservation   When Europeans started to settle in America fierce wars broke out between the settlers and the Indians who already lived there, over who the land belonged to. As the settlers moved further across the continent many thousands of Indians were killed and whole tribes were wiped out in the fighting. In the nineteenth century the United States government set aside areas of land called reservations for the Indians. There are 265 reservations in the United States today.

Tribe   There are hundreds of different Indian tribes living in America. Each tribe has it own language, culture and traditions which go back hundreds of years. Some of the more famous tribes include Apache, Blackfoot, Cherokee, Comanche, Hopi, Mohican, Navaho, Pueblo and Sioux Indians.

Jicarilla (Hik-a-ri-ya)   The Jicarilla Apache are one of six different groups of Apache. The Apache have always lived in the area called New Mexico. They are famous for their horsemanship.

Clan   There are two Jicarilla clans – the Olleros, or Reds and the Llaneros, or Whites. When a man marries, he joins his wife's clan.

Gojiya (Go-ji-ya)   On September 15th every year the Jicarilla Apache come together at Stone Lake to celebrate Gojiya. There is a feast to celebrate the food harvest and a ceremonial relay race. The young boys from both clans begin the relay race and later on the other men join in. When the Reds win, there will be plenty of animals and meat the following year. When the Whites win, there will be plenty of fruit and plant food. The Apache gods warned that if the Jicarilla stopped holding the race, they would starve.

Gods   The Jicarilla Apache believe that the gods are present everywhere in nature. No plant or animal life must ever be treated or used badly. Everything in the world is linked to a supreme god and his power can be used by man through ritual and ceremony.

Kiva   A kiva is a religious building where Indians worship. Two round kivas are built from tree branches at either end of the ceremonial race track. One kiva represents the sun and the other kiva represents the moon. The two clans worship in their separate kivas before and after the race.